My Spiritual Journey and Yours

by Nancy A. Waldron

Reggie

Introduction

This booklet arises out of my desire to share with you some of the ways I have found to more fully notice and experience the Sacred in my everyday life.

For many years I longed to gather all these little techniques together in one place and perhaps to share them with others.

So, in a simple way I have written about my process of how I go about enjoying the Sacred in my day-to-day life. I believe that sharing it with you helps expand my awareness, and perhaps will help you expand your awareness too.

Once I started this project, it kept growing as Spirit gave me ideas and insights. I know that if you start your own process there will be room for new concepts which inspire you. To create this opening I left space after each section to invite and encourage you to create and record your own process in your own words after each section. Take your time to reveal yourself, you know when it is right. I didn't realize the joy this process would awaken within me until I completed each section. Then I could see the magic in each step of my own journey.

There is a magic quality to this expansive approach to life and Spirit that inspires me daily.

I invite you to enjoy the journey along with me (and Reggie), and to create and write about your own Sacred magic in everyday life.

Nancy A. Waldron

My Sacred Space

Here is how I open, use, and close Sacred Space:

♥ Call in the four directions:
    North, South, East, West

♥ Call in above and below:
    Heaven and Earth

♥ Call in within and without:
    Conscious and Unconscious

♥ Invite the Highest Divine Beings throughout all of creation to assist me.

♥ Say, "I Open Sacred Space."

♥ Take a deep breath and visualize a flow of Energy from the Center of the Earth coming up through my feet to the top of my head.

♥ Take another deep breath and visualize the Grace of God flowing down into the top of my head, in, through and around me.

♥ Visualize *Pure Divine Golden Light* shielding me. Know that while it shields me, it protects me, surrounds me, and connects me.

♥ Visualize *Pure Divine White Light* clearing any dense or dark energy. Know that while it clears, it purifies all of the known and unknown parts of my self.

♥ Visualize *Pure Divine Crystal Clear Light* illuminating me. Know that while it illuminates, it expands and activates all that is the best and highest, the most Sacred and Holy within me.

♥ Visualize **_Pure Divine Rainbow Light_** radiating into my Beingness. Know that it radiates whatever color Lights I need. Know that my needs are known; all I have to do is be open and willing to receive.

♥ Meditate, ask God/Spirit to heal my self, my little Reggie, my family, strengthen my spiritual connection, pets, work, finances, relationships, or whatever I want help with. I take all the time I need.

♥ Thank and release the Highest Divine Beings throughout all of Creation.

♥ Say, "I close Sacred Space."

Reggie loves this energy and promptly goes to sleep by my feet or in his bed.

Your Sacred Space

♥ _____

_____

_____

_____

♥ _____

_____

_____

_____

♥ _____

_____

_____

_____

♥ _____

_____

_____

_____

♥ _____

_____

_____

_____

♥ _____

_____

_____

_____

♥ _____
_____
_____
_____

♥ _____
_____
_____
_____

♥ _____
_____
_____
_____

♥ _____
_____
_____
_____

♥ _____
_____
_____
_____

♥ _____
_____
_____
_____

My Body

♥ My body is a Sacred Temple, a gift from God.

♥ Enfold all aspects of my Beingness in Pure Divine Light all the time.

♥ Do my best to take good care of it with:
Positive Thoughts & Activities
Eat Healthy Food & Take Vitamins
Exercise & Walk (Reggie leads)
Rest (Reggie does lots of this)
Play (Reggie's favorite)

♥ Preventive measures include:
Massage Monthly (Reggie gets daily)
Chiropractic work, when warranted
Natural remedies, if possible
Western Medical, as needed

♥ Immediately meditate when I sense something is off, try to figure out the cause, what I need to do, and ask for God's/Spirit's help. Then wait to see what happens.

♥ Contact someone I trust, such as a family member, friend, spiritual advisor, or a personal Medium who communicates with Spirit, to assist with what needs to be done and what the underlying cause is. If appropriate, change my thoughts or actions. Over my lifetime, this process is the most helpful.

Your Body

♥ _____
_____
_____
_____

♥ _____
_____
_____
_____

♥ _____
_____
_____
_____

♥ _____
_____
_____
_____

♥ _____
_____
_____
_____

♥ _____
_____
_____
_____

My Garden Play

♥ Walk around my garden and tell all of it how beautiful it is, and how much I love every living thing, known and unknown. Tell it how grateful I am that it loves being in my garden, and that I enjoy the beauty, shade, fruit, and comfort it provides. I love the smells, sounds and colors.

♥ Before I had a garden, I found ways I could stay connected to the Earth and nature by going to the local park, putting a pot of flowers by my door or on the balcony, then later on my patio.

♥ Water whatever needs a little extra for the day, especially in the mid-summer. Reggie helps with everything, running in the bushes and around the trees, calling my attention to the little animals or birds, or digging for something known only to him.

♥ Trim dead flowers, branches, ivy that is out of control, grape vines that want to attach to anything but the wire, and take care of anything else that needs pruning, repotting, or a different place.

♥ Pick the fruit from my Peach, Apricot, Plum, or Tangerine Trees, then any Grapes that are ready.

♥ Ask to let me know if it needs something other than regular fertilizer.

♥ Sometimes I lean against one of the strong trees and ask it to give me some of its strength and solidity.

♥ The fairies, elves, and little sprites play in the mini-woods and send forth such lightness it makes me smile.

♥ Bliss lights send green twinkling light throughout at night giving it a mystical feel and look. I invite it to play.

♥ Visualize sparkling Divine Rainbow Light showering down, blessing all as it rests during the night.

Your Garden Play

♥ _____

_____

_____

_____

♥ _____

_____

_____

_____

♥ _____

_____

_____

_____

♥ _____

_____

_____

_____

♥ _____

_____

_____

_____

♥ _____

_____

_____

_____

My Porch Time

♥ Mornings, afternoons, and evenings I like to sit on my backyard porch in my outdoor rocking chair with my feet up in another chair and have MY TIME.

♥ This is the time where I do not let anything interfere with MY TIME, unless I CHOOSE to do so. Reggie likes this time.

♥ I sit and look out at my garden enjoying it all – the birds, butterflies, the squirrels, the wee ones. I allow this energy into my space and let it entertain, soothe, and renew me.

♥ I read The Bible, other spiritual books, romance novels, or whatever magazine calls to me.

♥ There is a vibration and frequency to everything. At times I can feel the differences as I focus on each thing. I am so grateful for this awareness.

♥ Some days, I stay on the porch most of the day as I love being outside in the fresh air, surrounded by beautiful foliage, caressed by a breeze. I let myself float and become the breeze or the tree or a bird or whatever.

♥ I allow Nature to take me to a place of peace, of connection with the spirits, of connection with God to renew my Soul. Reggie is so peaceful out there.

♥ When I go inside after my Porch Time, I am at peace. I am filled with deep love and gratitude. I go on in joy.

Your Time

♥ _____

_____

_____

_____

♥ _____

_____

_____

_____

♥ _____

_____

_____

_____

♥ _____

_____

_____

_____

♥ _____

_____

_____

_____

♥ _____

_____

_____

_____

Situation Techniques

♥ In *non-personal situations* like watching the news, hearing a police siren, seeing an ambulance or a dead animal along the roadside, hearing an argument not involving me, and other disturbing situations:

> Immediately send Pure Divine Sparking Rainbow Light. The "sparking" breaks up the energy and the other lights are used for whatever is needed. I use "Light" as it is shorter and God/Spirit knows my intent.

> For instance, when I watch the news, listen to the negativity of some situation, I immediately send Pure Divine Sparking Rainbow Light through the TV to the situation and all effected by it in any way, to the owners/producers/staff of the TV station, and to all the millions of people watching it.

♥ If I have a *personal situation*, I know on some level I chose to create it. It may be a financial issue, a relationship issue, a work issue, a health issue, or any personal issue. I may do all of the following immediately, or one or two:

> Immediately take action to assess my part, whether that is send payment or make a phone call, apologize in person or by phone as soon as I become aware I was out of spiritual alignment, talk to my boss directly to resolve the work issue, address the health issue head-on with qualified people, etc.

> Meditate, ask for God's/Spirit's assistance, and wait a bit to see what happens, then act. Reggie comes close to comfort me.

> Contact a Medium who communicates with Spirit to get a spiritual view of action and cause, and/or share with a trusted family member or friend. Contact a professional for further assistance.

♥ Every step of the way, I say: "I choose to...." I own my thoughts and actions.

Your Situation Techniques

♥ _____

_____

_____

_____

♥ _____

_____

_____

_____

♥ _____

_____

_____

_____

♥ _____

_____

_____

_____

♥ _____

_____

_____

_____

♥ _____

_____

_____

_____

Prayers Along the Way

♥ Morning Walk:
Silently I say, "Good Morning All That Is, I love you. Bless this land, this city, this State, the Nation, the World, the Earth, and All That Is."

Then I open Sacred Space and silently ask for healing or whatever assistance is needed for my little Reggie, my close and extended family, my friends, my fellow dancers, my church family, the groups, all the kingdoms (plant, animal, mineral, etc.), the Earth and All That Is. Then I close Sacred Space.

♥ Running Errands/Trips:
In my car, I silently say, "Bless everyone I pass this and every day with infinite blessings now and forevermore." Reggie blesses everyone with his tongue wagging and his head out the car window.

In the grocery store, I silently say, "Thank you for this great abundance of more than I need and for all who helped to provide it. Thank you for the money to buy what I need."

On a trip, I silently say, "Thank you for the competent drivers, the perfectly operating vehicles, the smooth roadway, the good weather conditions, the open flow of traffic, and the beautiful scenery. Thank you for making this trip interesting, easy, and time passing quickly."

♥ Meals:
At home or in a restaurant, I silently say, "Thank you for this wonderful food and all in the chain who had any part in providing or preparing it. I am so grateful for all known and unknown blessings." Reggie says thank you by instantly eating everything on his plate.

♥ Night:
Just before I go to sleep, I say the Lord's Prayer and thank God for Reggie, my family, friends, and all of the blessings, known and unknown to me this day. Reggie lays his little body next to mine and we go to sleep.

Your Prayers

♥ _____

_____

_____

_____

_____

_____

♥ _____

_____

_____

_____

_____

_____

♥ _____

_____

_____

_____

_____

_____

♥ _____

_____

_____

_____

_____

_____

My Self Talk

♥ I brought highly emotional language and labels into my adult life. There were many colorful adjectives. It wasn't just a dog or cat walking by – it was a miserable, no good, lazy, worthless piece of _____. Learned, judgmental language and labels in home, media, work, etc., can limit and harm me and society. Labels are necessary for identification of certain things and in certain places.

♥ If something needs to be addressed, I do it directly without the adjectives and negativity. My language and self talk change with experience, classes, and spiritual growth. I own my words!

I used to say:	Now I say:
I should...	I choose...
It's hard.	It is an opportunity.
I always/never...	Right now, I...
I judge...	I assess...
She is good/bad.	She is loveable.
He is old/dumb.	He is knowable.

♥ I have learned to keep it in the present; this moment is all I have. I keep it soft and kind as I am thinking or speaking about myself, someone, or something else. Each is a part of the sacred All That Is. I want to harm none. Reggie loves my soft, sweet talk to him and gives me kisses.

♥ Thoughts are things, so I choose soft and kind ones for myself and others. A saying that helped me change is:

What I think about – I bring about.

Your Self Talk

♥ Old Self Talk: _____

_____

_____

_____

♥ _____

_____

_____

_____

I used to say:

_____

_____

_____

_____

_____

_____

Now I say:

_____

_____

_____

_____

_____

_____

♥ New Self Talk: _____

_____

_____

_____

♥ _____

_____

_____

_____

My Sexuality

♥ **Mental.** My mind has to "know" that the One I make love with likes and loves all aspects of my beingness. This includes who I am and what I do as a Spiritual Being, how I am physically, that I have keen awareness of our emotional connection, and that everything is held as a Divine Connection.

♥ **Physical.** My body loves being kissed, touched, held, caressed, and making love with The One I love. I hold my body as a sacred temple, a gift from God, to be cherished.

♥ **Emotional.** The feeling of being loved for who I am, how I look, act, and behave is one of the greatest joys of my life. That someone gets the essence of me uplifts me to a very high sacred place. My heart opens wide with love.

♥ **Spiritual.** The closest sacred connection I have in this life is through making love. When all parts of me open to join with my love, my soul connects with Divine Love. It feels like a blessing from God upon our love expressed through the sexual act.

Your Sexuality

♥ Mental _____

_____

_____

_____

_____

_____

♥ Physical _____

_____

_____

_____

_____

_____

♥ Emotional _____

_____

_____

_____

_____

_____

♥ Spiritual _____

_____

_____

_____

_____

_____

My Reminders Along the Way

♥ I made a list of reminders that help me to stay on my spiritual path, to do the best I can on a daily basis, and to honor God in all. My priorities are God, myself, Reggie (dog), my spiritual work, our families, and all others (humans, plants, animals, minerals, visibles and invisibles, known and unknown). With authenticity, kindness, compassion, and genuine love, I remind myself to:

1.   Consciously stay aware of and clearly receive God's/ Spirit's guidance personally and in my spiritual work.

2.   Obey and uphold the laws of the Universe, as well as actively uphold the appropriate laws of my country, and stay politically aware.

3.   Respect myself and others, affirm others and avoid uncaring criticism, hateful words, physical attacks, and self-destructive behavior.

4.   Share my feelings honestly as soon as I become aware of them, express my anger in safe ways, and work to solve problems peacefully.

5.   Listen carefully to others, especially those who disagree with me, and consider other's feelings and needs for understanding.

6.   Promptly apologize and make amends when I have hurt another, forgive myself and others, and do not hold grudges.

7.   Treat the environment and all living things, including our pets, with respect, tenderness, and care.

8.   Financially be responsible, pay my bills on time, save, and donate to others.

9.   Select entertainment, games, and activities that support my values and avoid anything that makes violence, explicit

sexuality, abuse, overt or covert undermining of the character integrity, or morals of individuals or society look exciting, funny, or acceptable.

10.   Challenge violence, abuse, and other inappropriate subjects in all their forms whenever I encounter them, whether it be at home, at a spiritual gathering, at work or in the community, and assist others who are treated unfairly.

11.   Meditate, journal, and/or read spiritual material daily, balance play and work, and take time for myself.

12.   Hold my inner self to a higher standard, outwardly conduct myself with grace, dignity and humor, create joy, beauty and peace in my home and life.

Your Reminders Along the Way

1 _____

_____

_____

_____

2 _____

_____

_____

_____

3 _____

_____

_____

_____

4 _____

_____

_____

_____

5 _____

_____

_____

_____

6 _____

_____

_____

_____

7 _____

_____

_____

_____

8 _____

_____

_____

_____

9 _____

_____

_____

_____

10 _____

_____

_____

_____

11 _____

_____

_____

_____

12 _____

_____

_____

_____

My Environment

If I do not have this beautiful Earth to live on, what does anything else matter – not power, money, work, or anything else.

♥ **Bless the Earth.** Each day I start with blessing the Earth and All That Is. I give thanks for all of it – the beauty of the mountains, rivers, trees, grasses, flowers, the abundance, the seasons and rhythm of the Earth systems – the weather, the water, the air, the fire, the flow, the rotation.

♥ **Take Care of the Earth.** Everything gets reduced, reused or recycled. I save water bottles, papers, nails, and other things I find for reuse. I put all my trash in appropriate bins. I grow organic and rarely use chemicals. I pick up trash along my streets and put it in the designated container. I have a trash bag in my car and throw nothing out. A church I attended committed to picking up trash for miles along an Interstate highway. I throw nothing in any river, lake, ocean, or water body.

♥ **Reduce Pollution.** I combine trips to the Post Office, grocery store, and pet store to save gas. I take my reusable bags to the grocery store, and skip bags when I have one or two items at other stores. My neighbor suggested we combine our trash to save the Trash Truck an extra stop, thereby reducing pollution, gas, brakes, etc. Ride a bicycle, buy a gas-efficient, pollution-reducing vehicle, and keep abreast of new ways to reduce pollution – solar, wind, and water generators. Share rides. Reduce noise pollution. Use less heat and air conditioning. Buy energy efficient products. Turn off lights. Buy LED bulbs. I stopped smoking, thus reducing air pollution and saving my life.

♥ **Build/Repair Green.** When repairs were needed for my home, I requested products be used that were green wherever possible. New residential and commercial structures are being built green. Tiny homes are being built to offer less stressful, more Earth-saving, and efficient living.

I explore ways to help save the Earth – my home.

Your Environment

♥ Bless the Earth _____

_____

_____

_____

_____

_____

♥ Take Care of the Earth _____

_____

_____

_____

_____

_____

♥ Reduce Pollution _____

_____

_____

_____

_____

_____

♥ Build/Repair Green _____

_____

_____

_____

_____

_____

Every Moment

of

Every Day

is

Sacred

Nancy A. Waldron
www.nancyawaldron.com
530.878.5757 | nancyawaldron@aol.com

www.ingramcontent.com/pod-product-compliance
Lightning Source LLC
Chambersburg PA
CBHW060558100426
42742CB00013B/2609